Jacques OFFENBACH

OVERTURE
for
Orphée aux enfers
Arranged by
CARL BINDER
Edited by
Clark McAlister
(1860)

Study Score
Partitur

SERENISSIMA MUSIC, INC.

ORCHESTRA

2 Flutes (2nd also Piccolo)

2 Oboes

2 Clarinets in A

2 Bassoons

4 Horns in F

2 Trumpets in F

3 Trombones

Tuba

Timpani

Percussion
(Triangle, Cymbals, Bass Drum)

Harp

Violins I

Violins II

Violas

Violoncellos

Double Basses

This overture was arranged by Carl Binder on themes from Offenbach's 1858 operetta *Orphée aux enfers* for the Vienna premiere.

Duration: ca.9 minutes
First performance: March 17, 1860
Vienna, Carl-Theatrer
Vienna premiere of *Orphée aux enfers*
Carl Binder (conductor)

© Copyright 2008 Clark McAlister
All rights reserved.

ISMN: 979-0-58042-076-3
Previously issued by E.F. Kalmus as A1869

Overture
on Motives from the Operetta
Orpheus in the Underworld

JACQUES OFFENBACH
Compiled and Arranged by Carl Binder
Edited by Clark McAlister

* Flute2/Piccolo, Cymbals and Bass Drum are optional. They do not appear in Binder's original score.

Copyright ©2005 Clark McAlister.

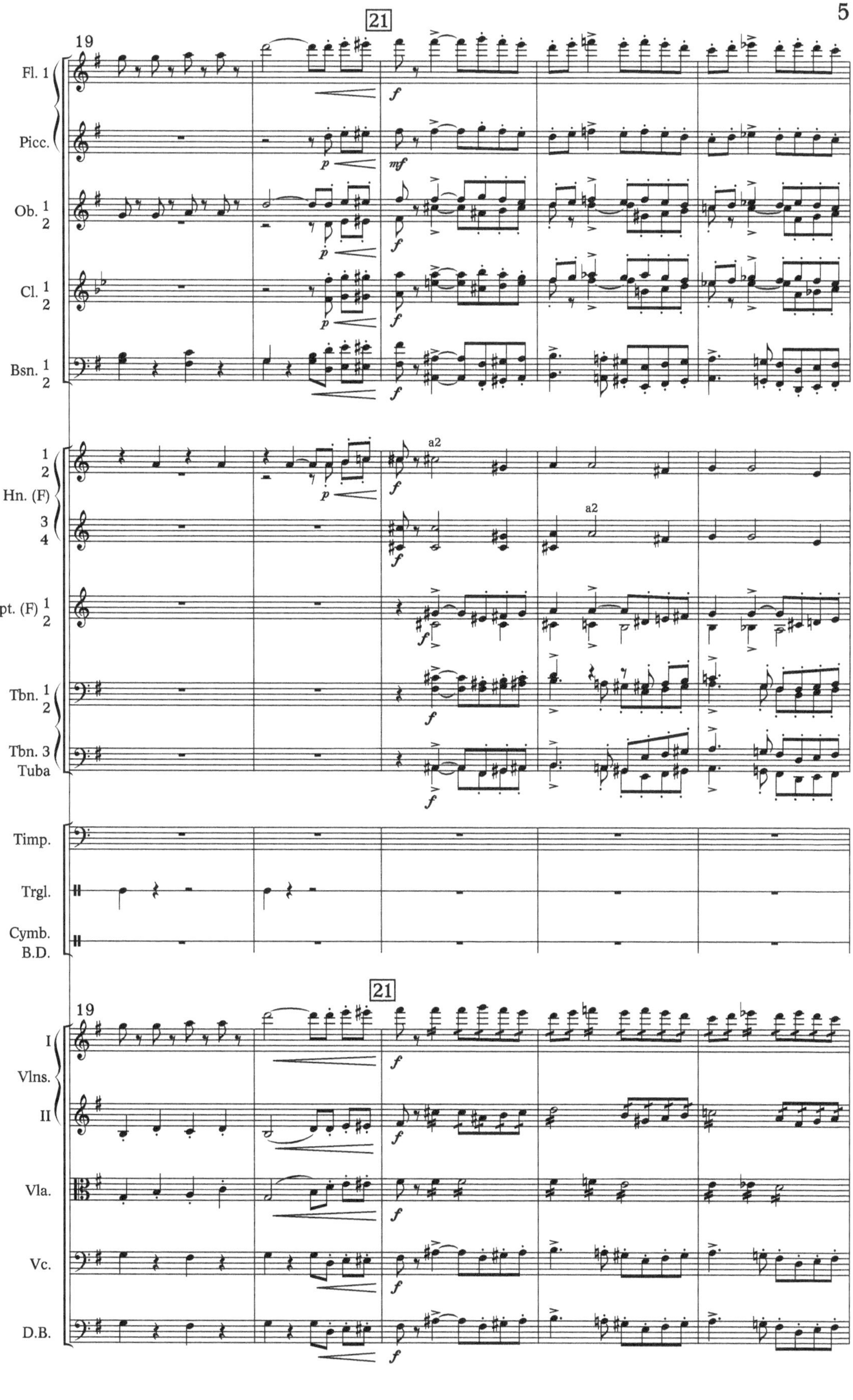

19
21
Fl. 1
Picc.
Ob. 1 2
Cl. 1 2
Bsn. 1 2
Hn. (F) 1 2 3 4
Tpt. (F) 1 2
Tbn. 1 2
Tbn. 3 Tuba
Timp.
Trgl.
Cymb. B.D.
Vlns. I II
Vla.
Vc.
D.B.
a2
f
mf
p

*Viola, mm. 47–72: small notes to be played in absence of Harp, without mutes.

** Vln. I, mm. 60–68: small notes to be played also, in absence of Harp
*** Vln. II, mm. 60–68: small notes (lower staff) to be played also, in absence of Harp.

* Vc. solo: Play in absence of Harp.

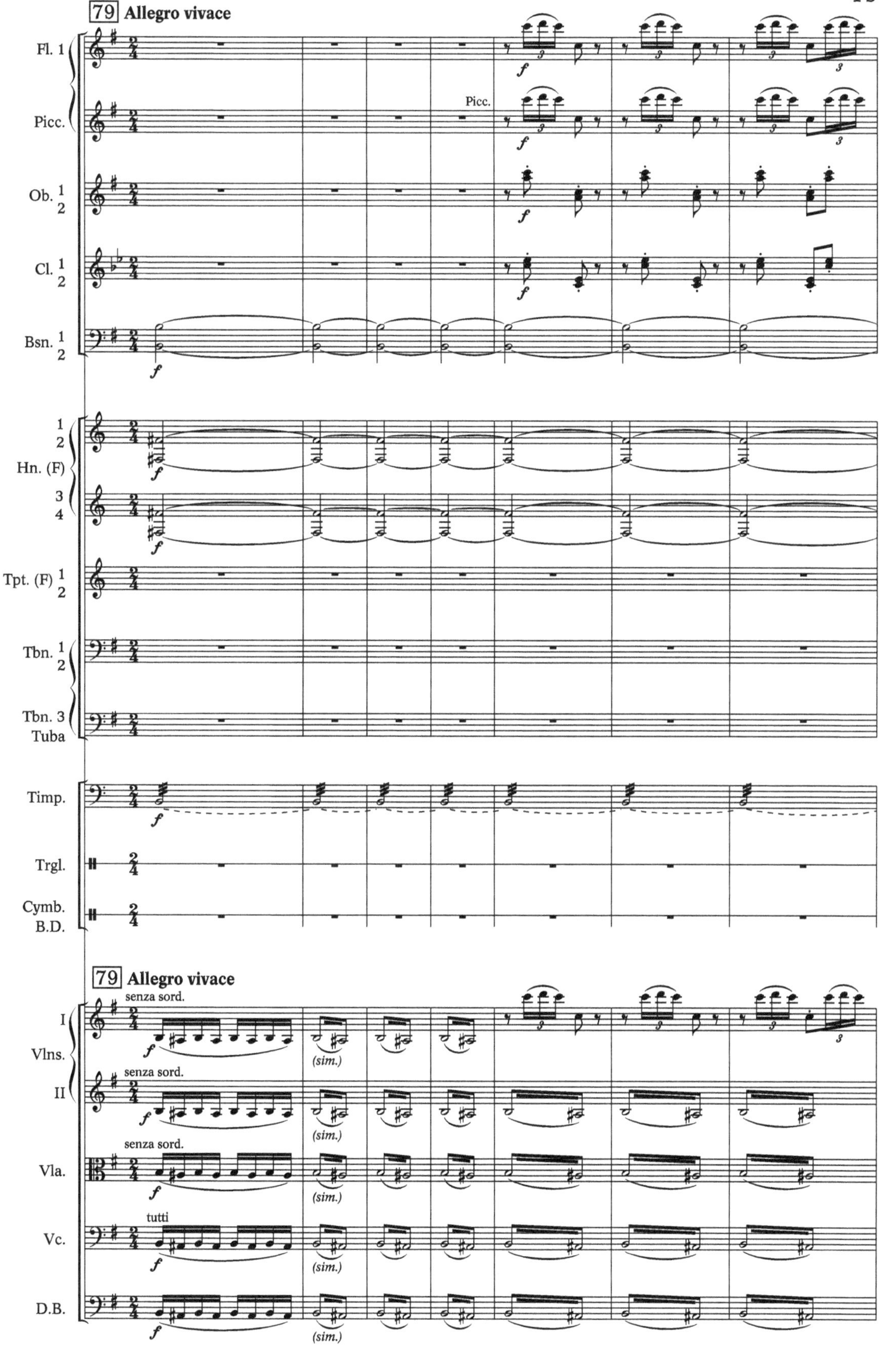
79 Allegro vivace
Fl. 1
Picc.
Picc.
Ob. 1 2
Cl. 1 2
Bsn. 1 2
Hn. (F) 1 2 3 4
Tpt. (F) 1 2
Tbn. 1 2
Tbn. 3 Tuba
Timp.
Trgl.
Cymb. B.D.
79 Allegro vivace
senza sord.
I
Vlns.
II
senza sord.
(sim.)
senza sord.
Vla.
(sim.)
tutti
Vc.
(sim.)
D.B.
(sim.)

20

22

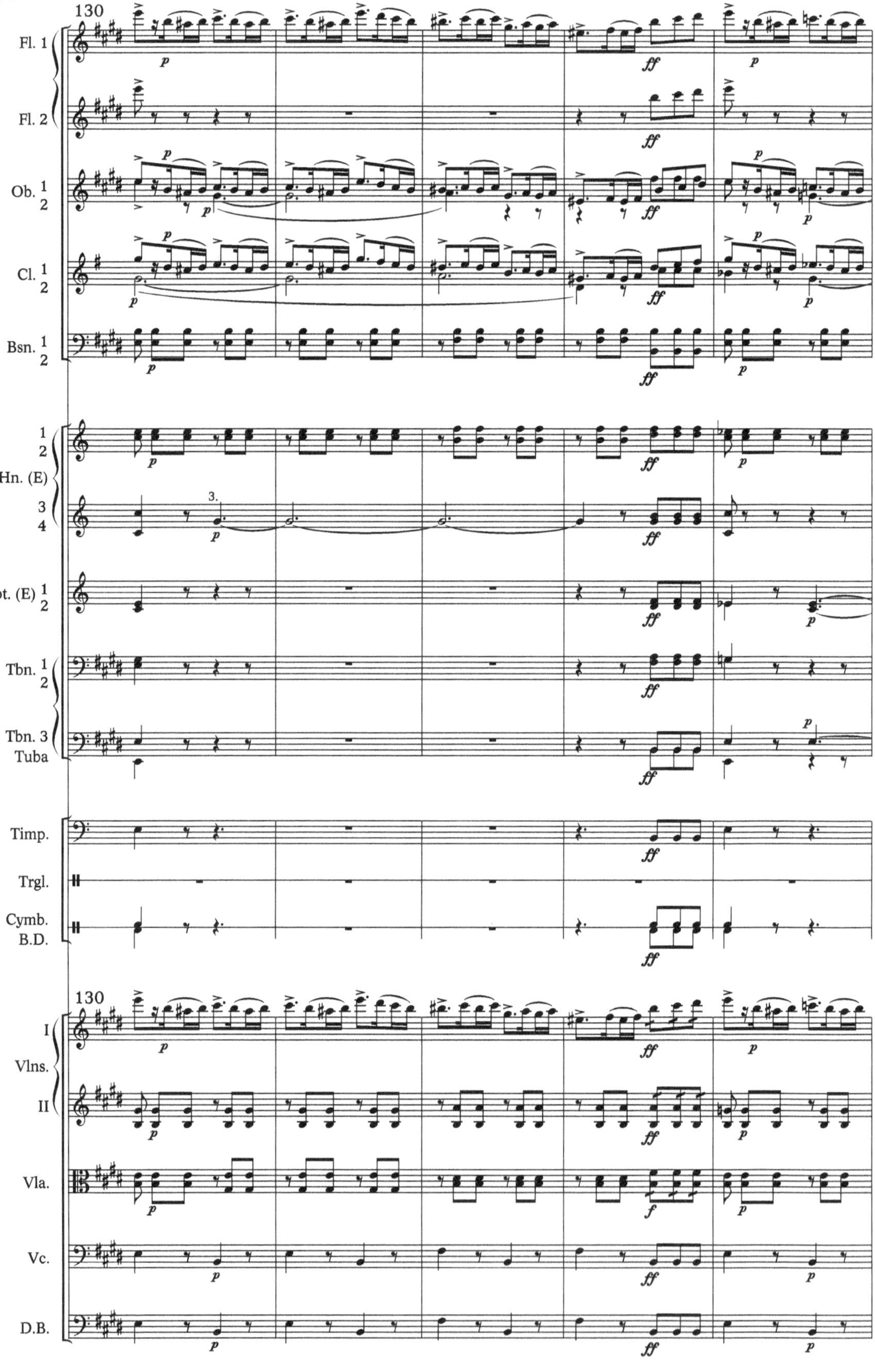
130
Fl. 1
Fl. 2
Ob. 1 2
Cl. 1 2
Bsn. 1 2
Hn. (E) 1 2
3 4
3.
Tpt. (E) 1 2
Tbn. 1 2
Tbn. 3 Tuba
Timp.
Trgl.
Cymb. B.D.
130
Vlns. I
II
Vla.
Vc.
D.B.

25

26

30

38

43